# ON THE WATER

## GRAYSCALE COLORING BOOK FOR ADULTS

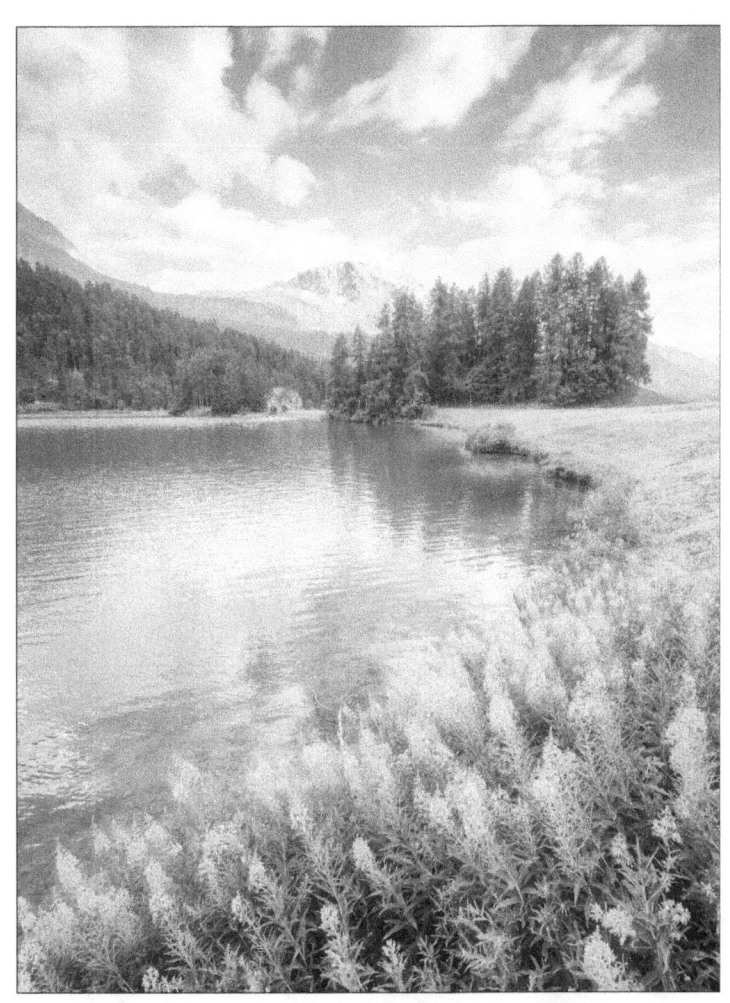

*Majestic* **COLORING**

ISBN: 978-1534958333

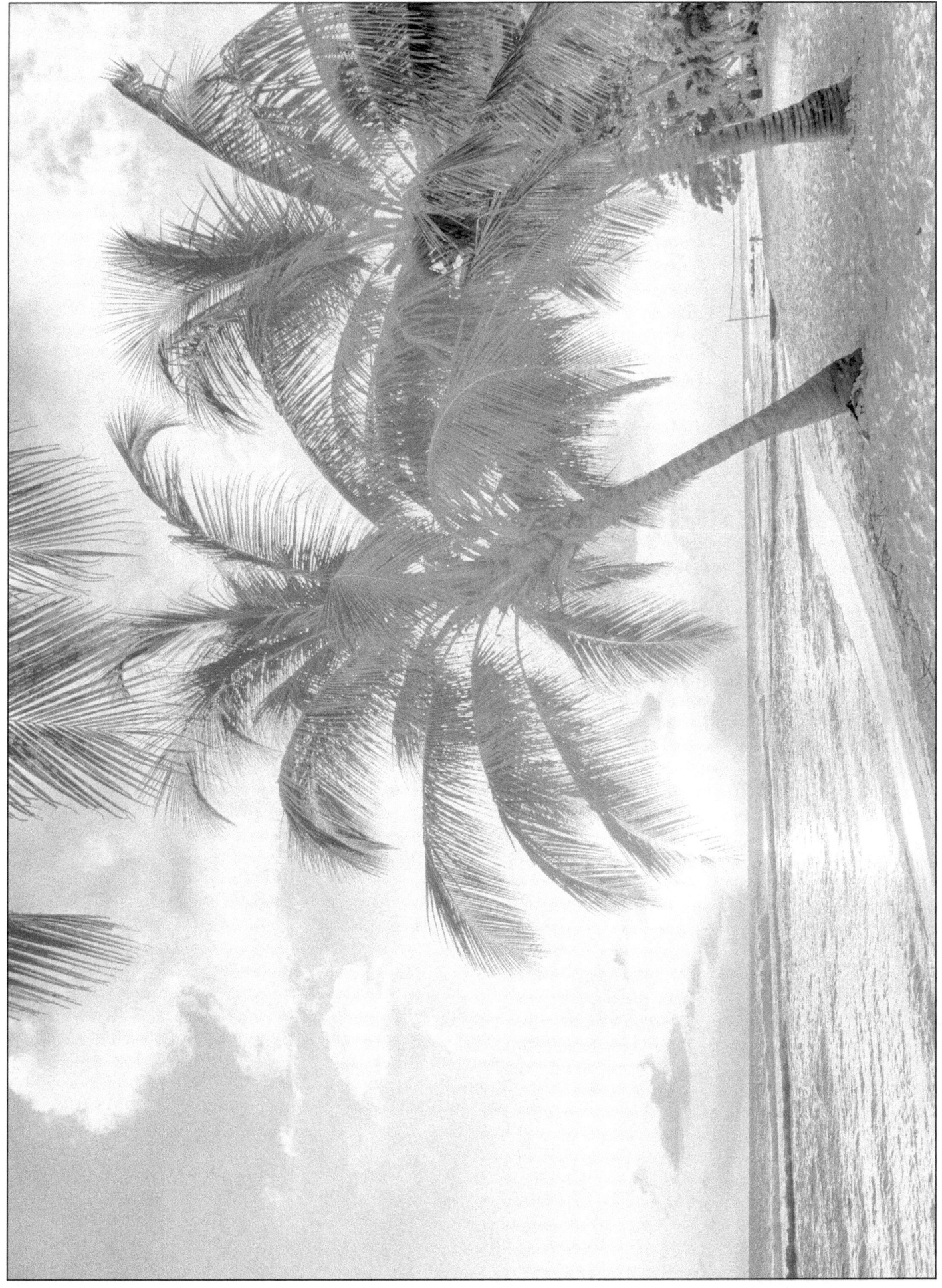

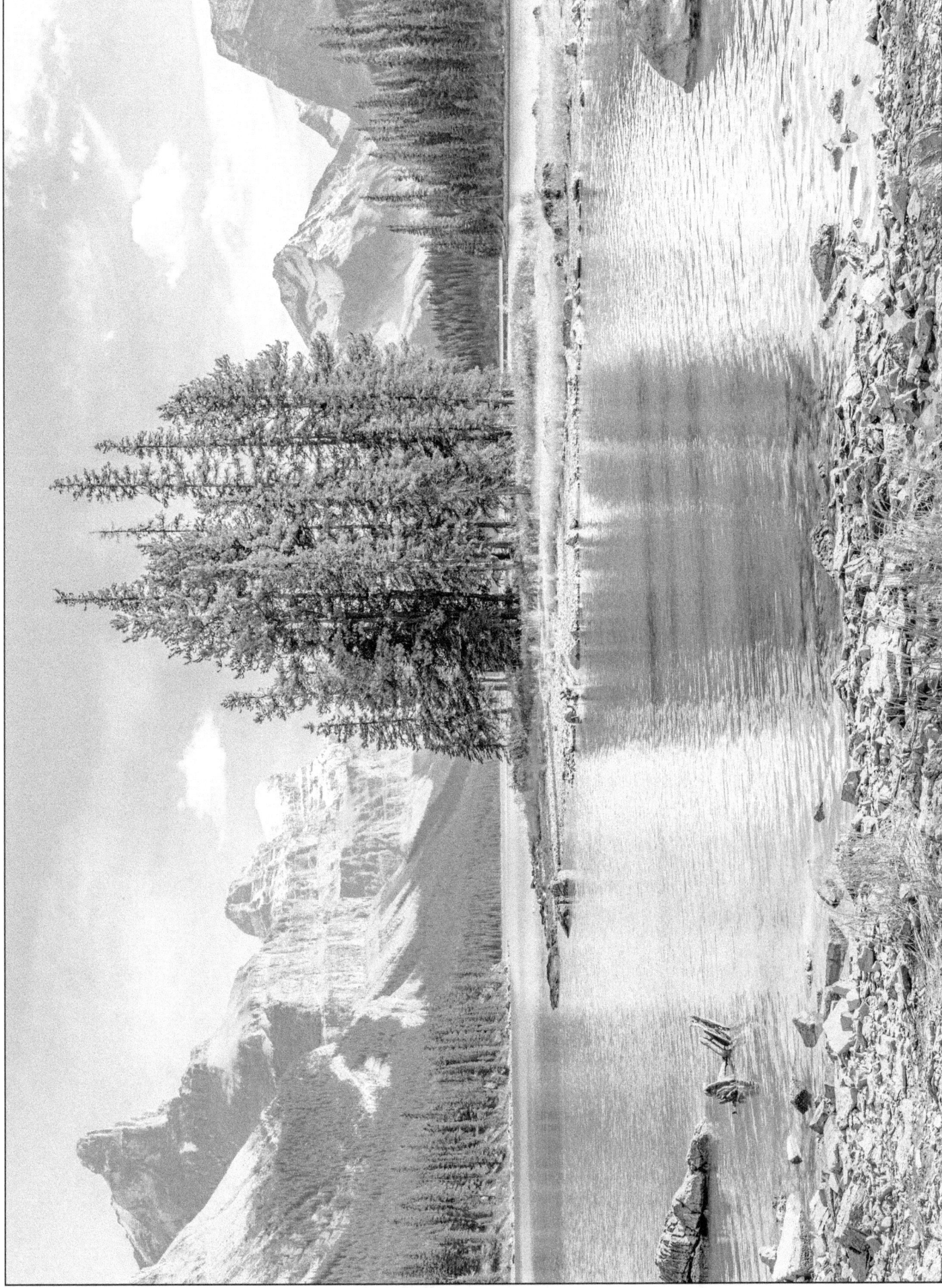

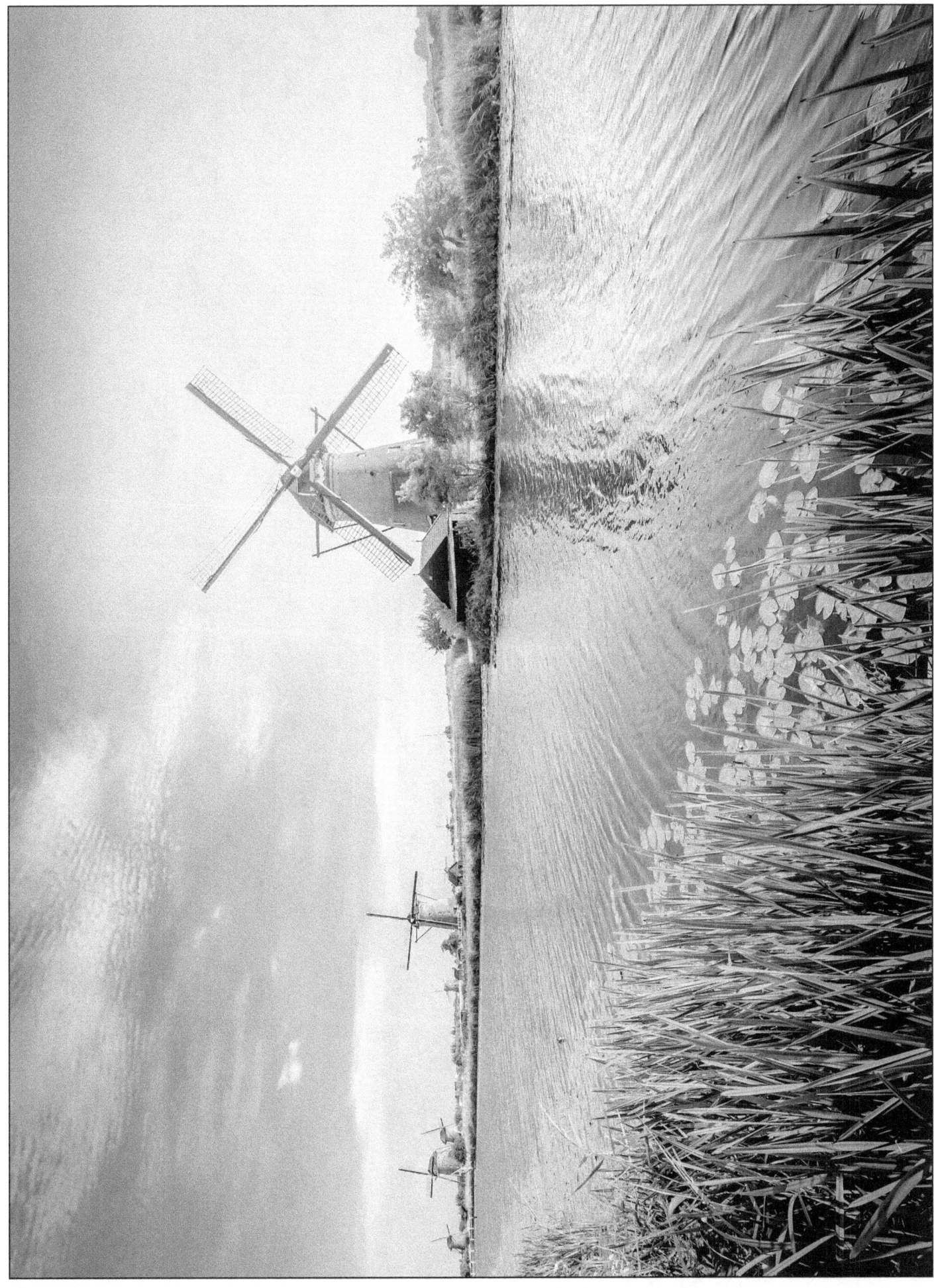

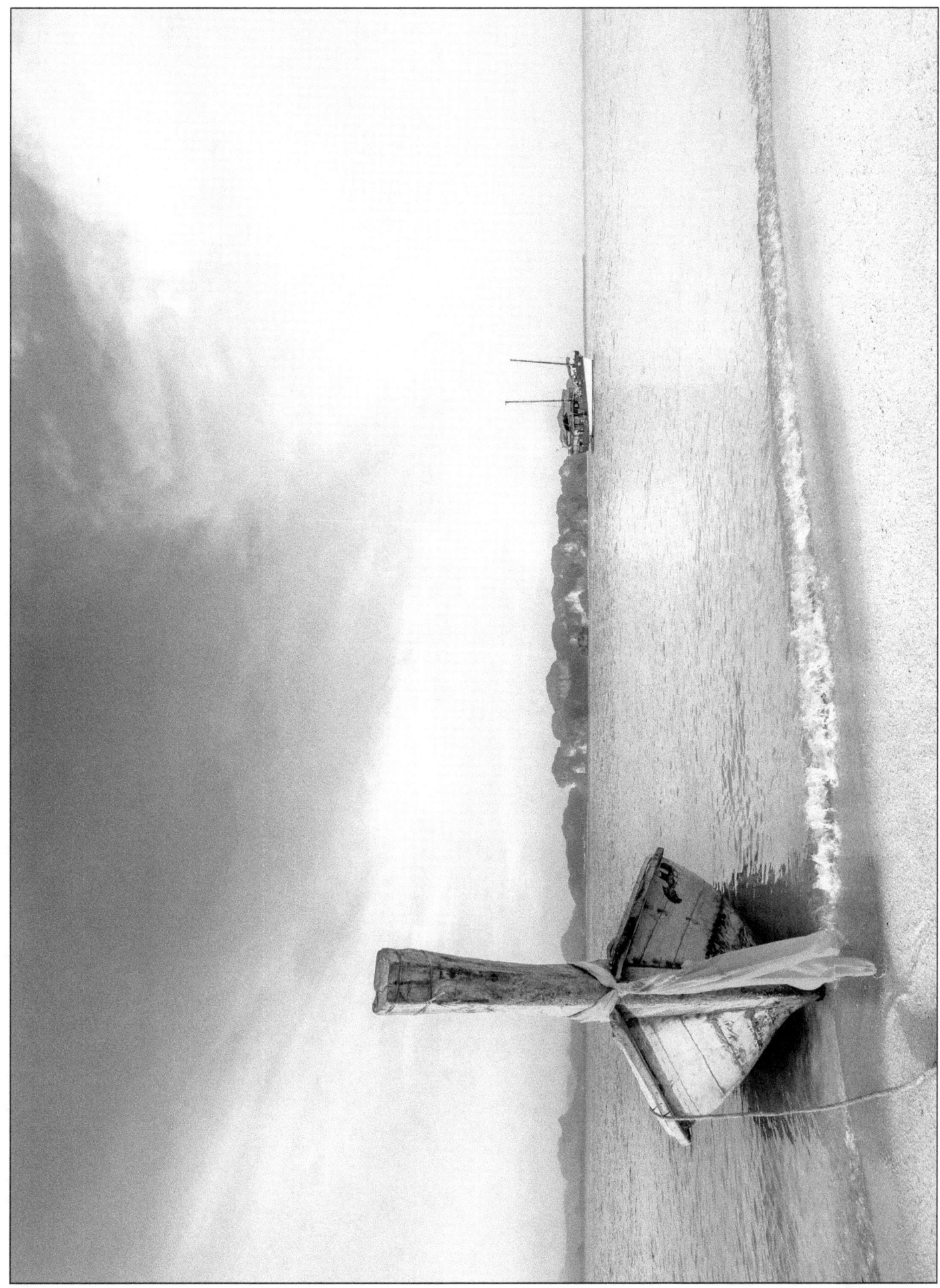

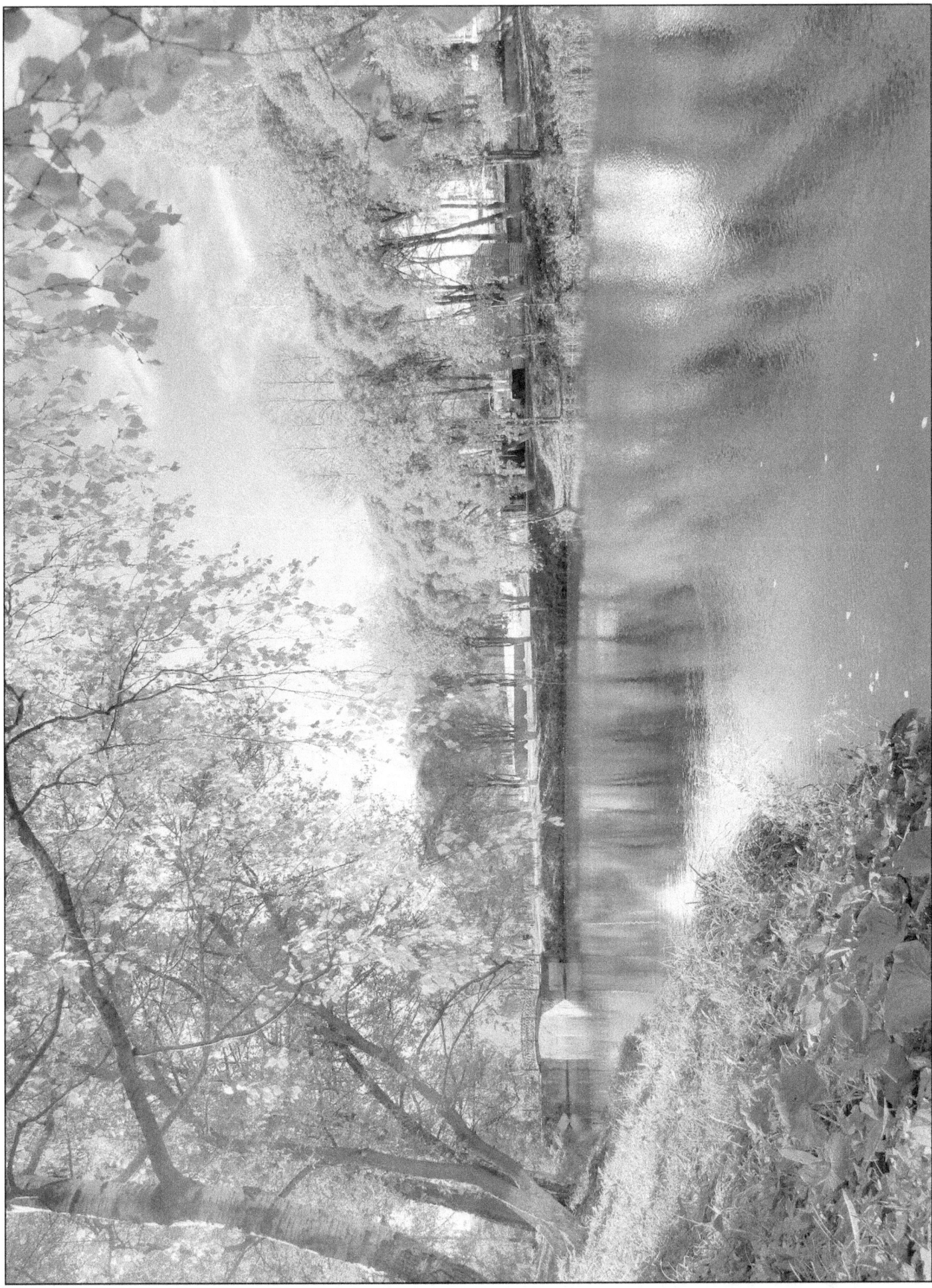

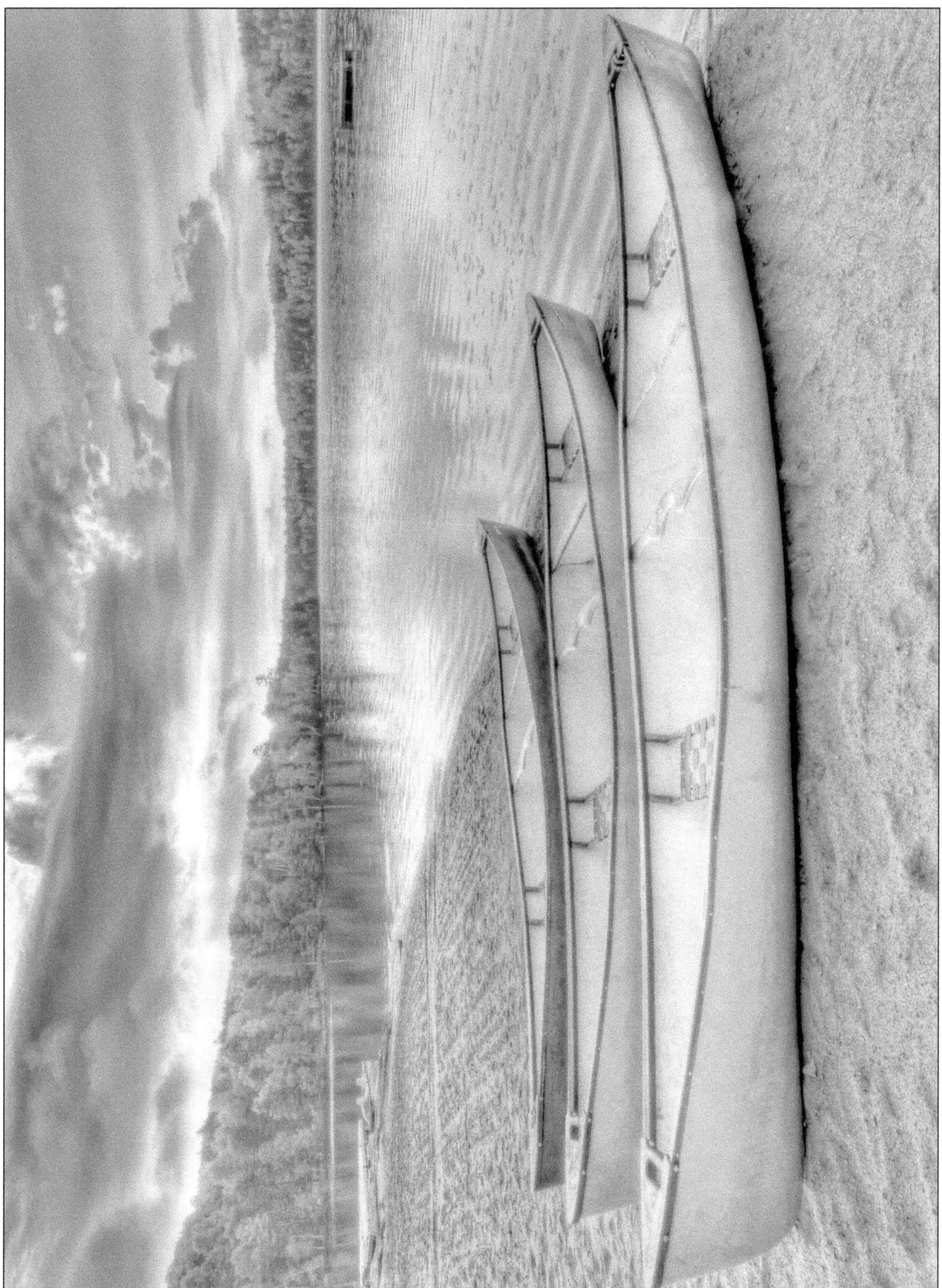

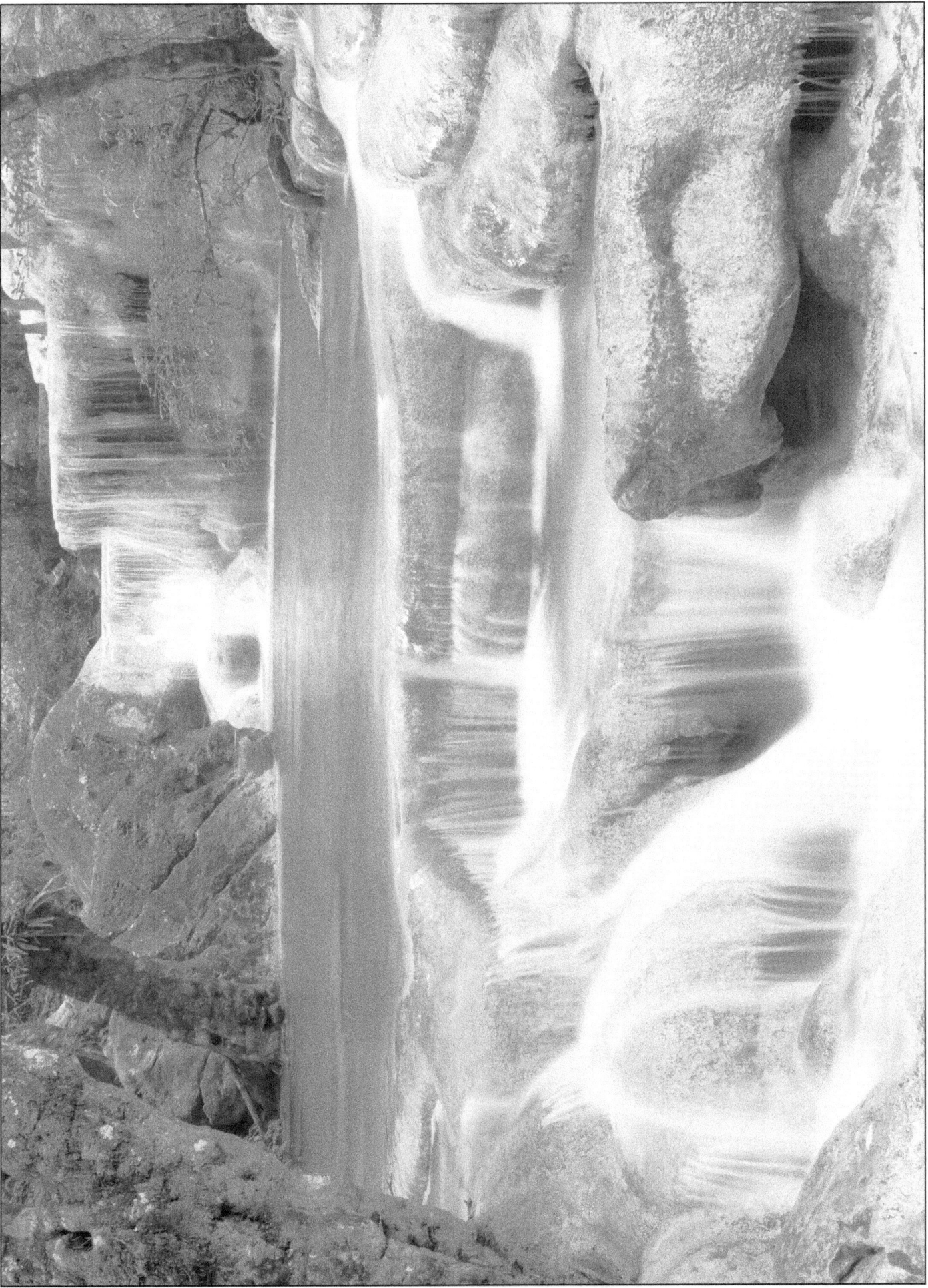

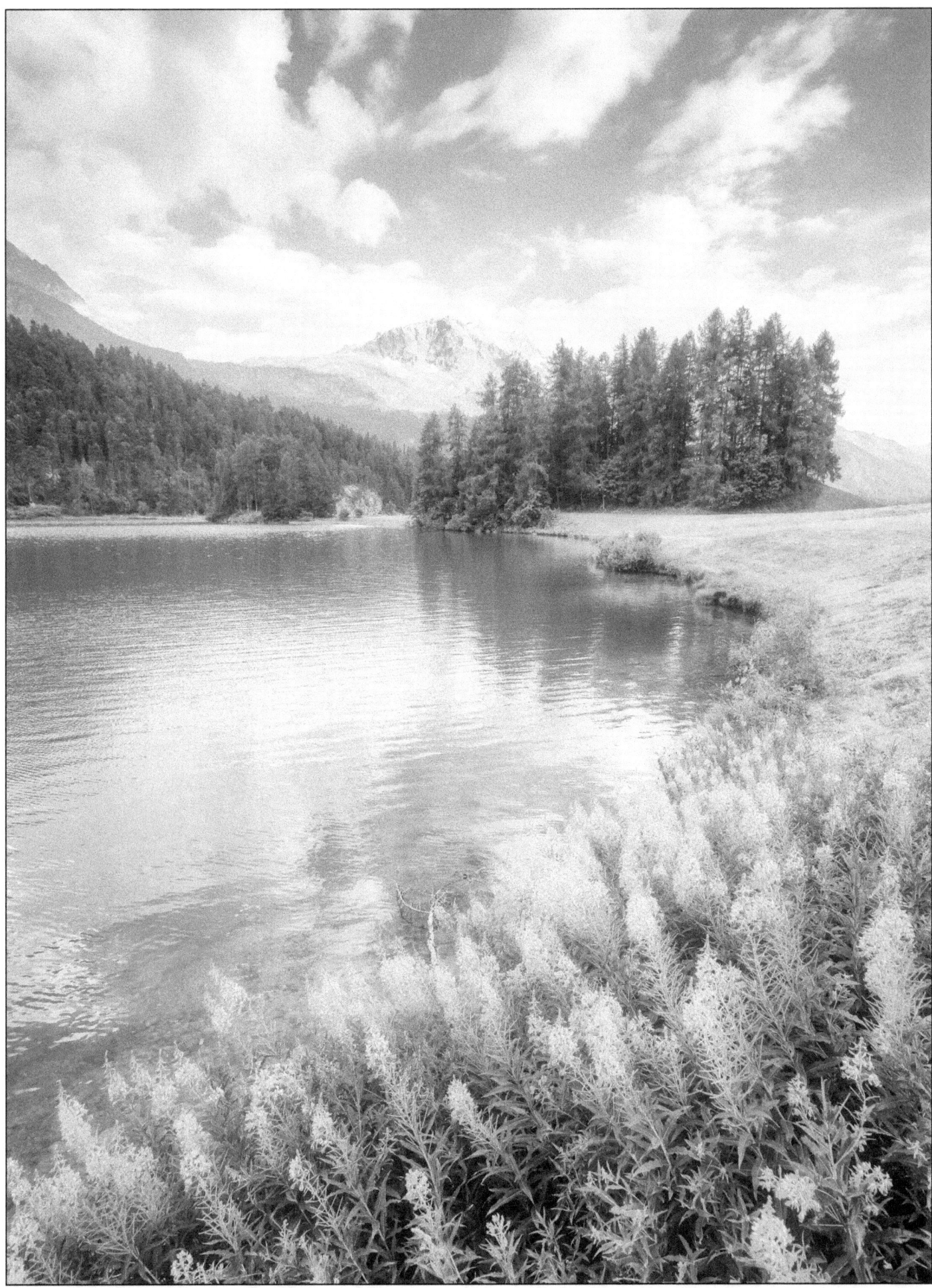

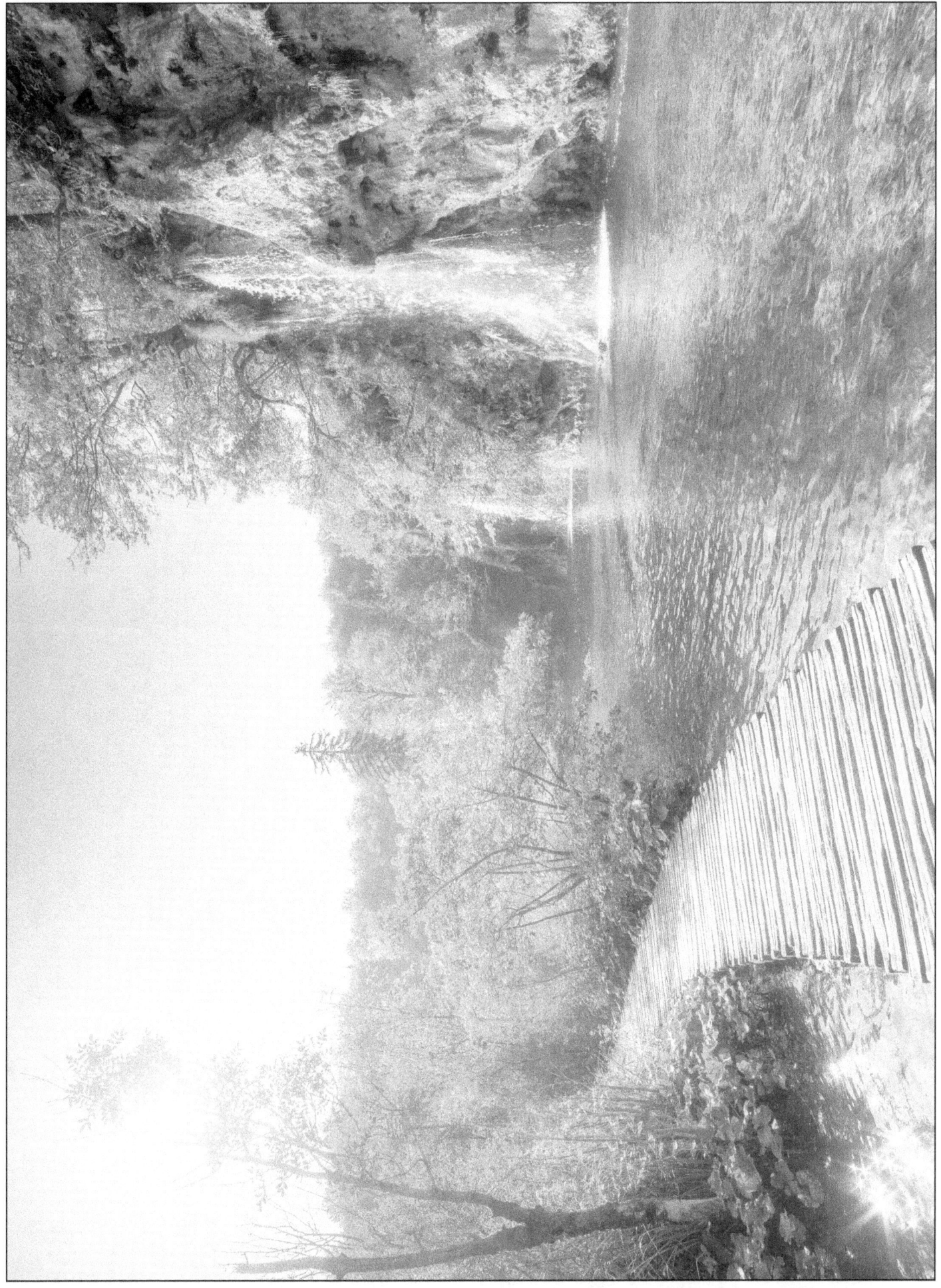

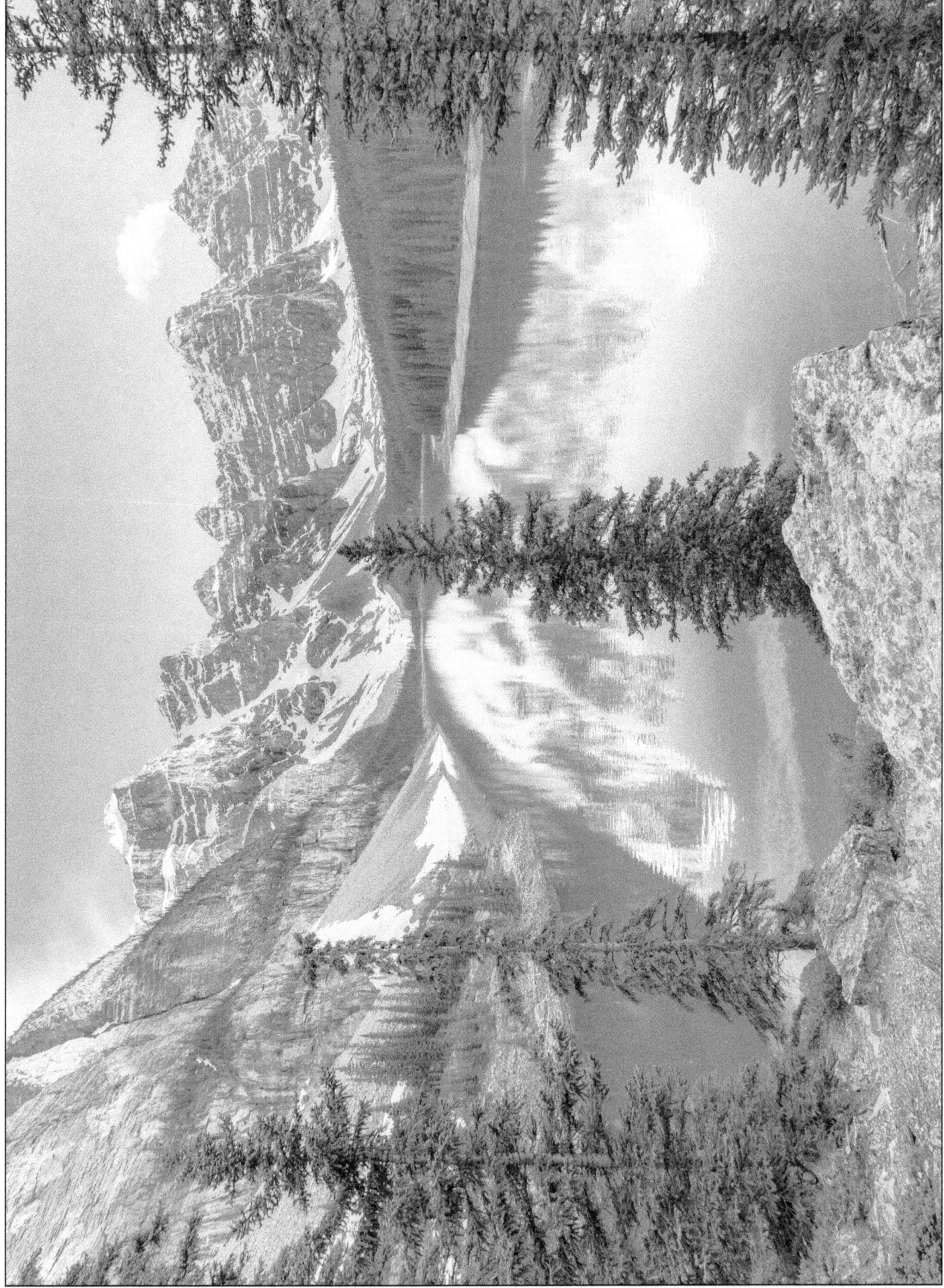

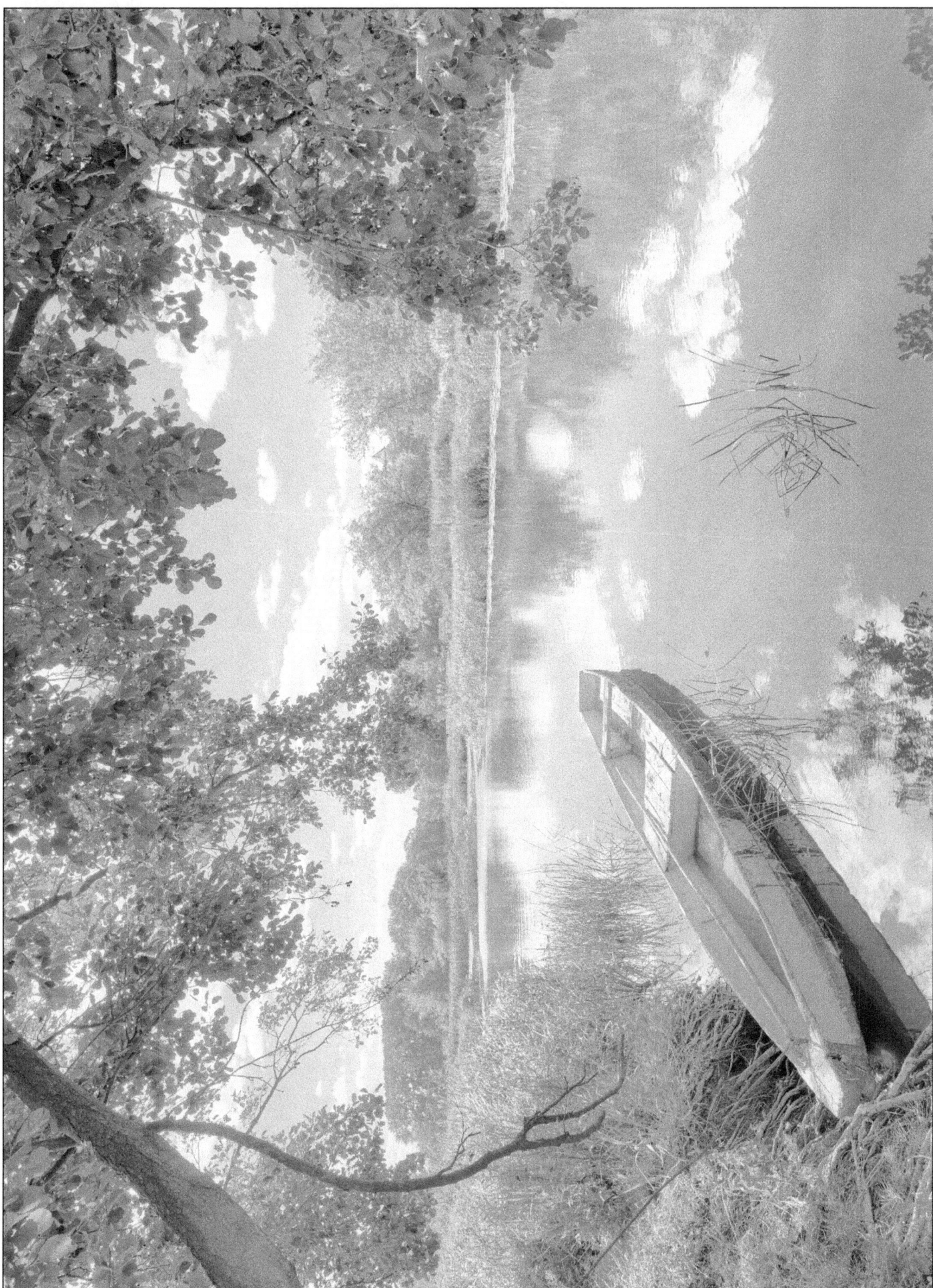

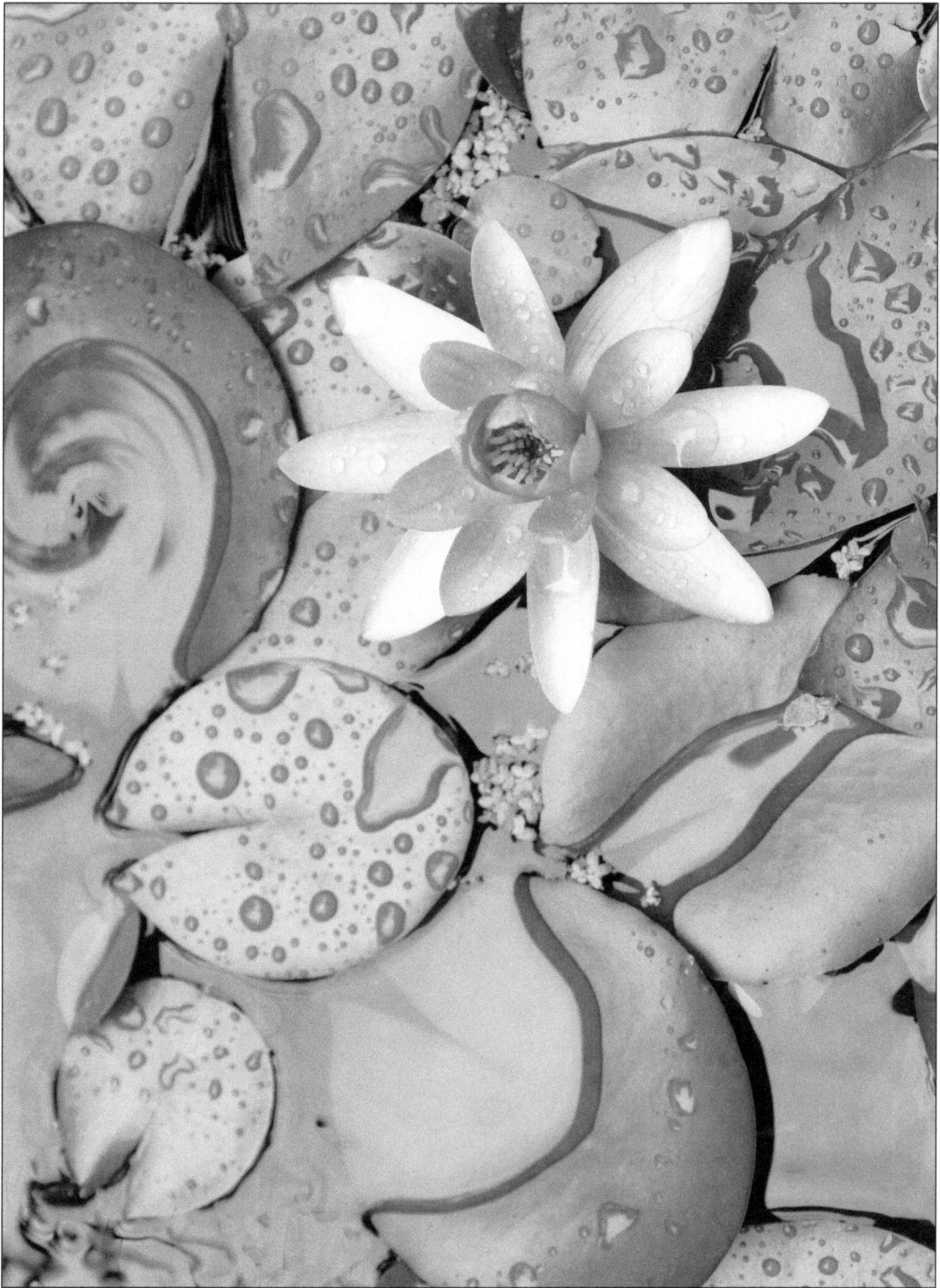

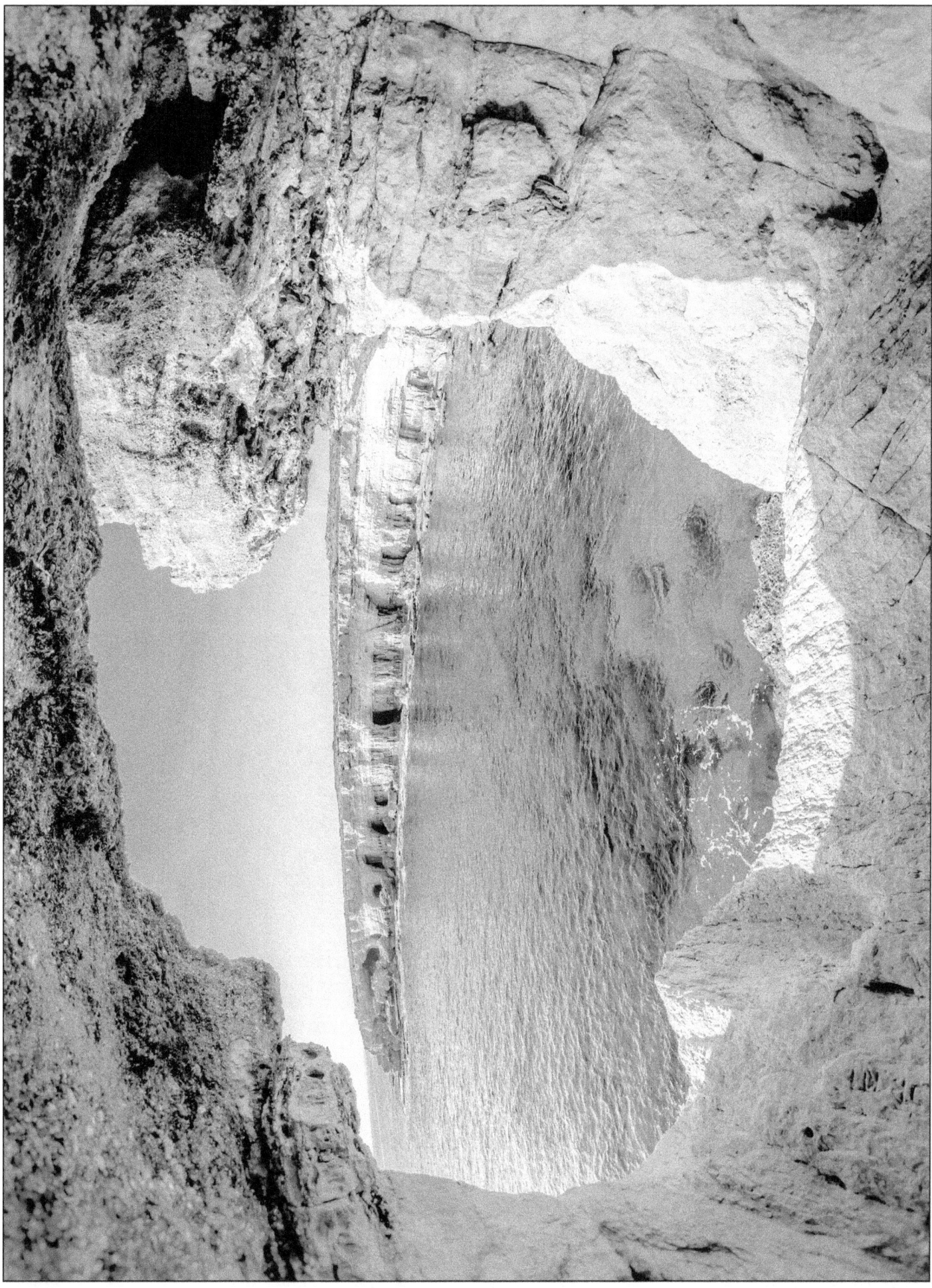

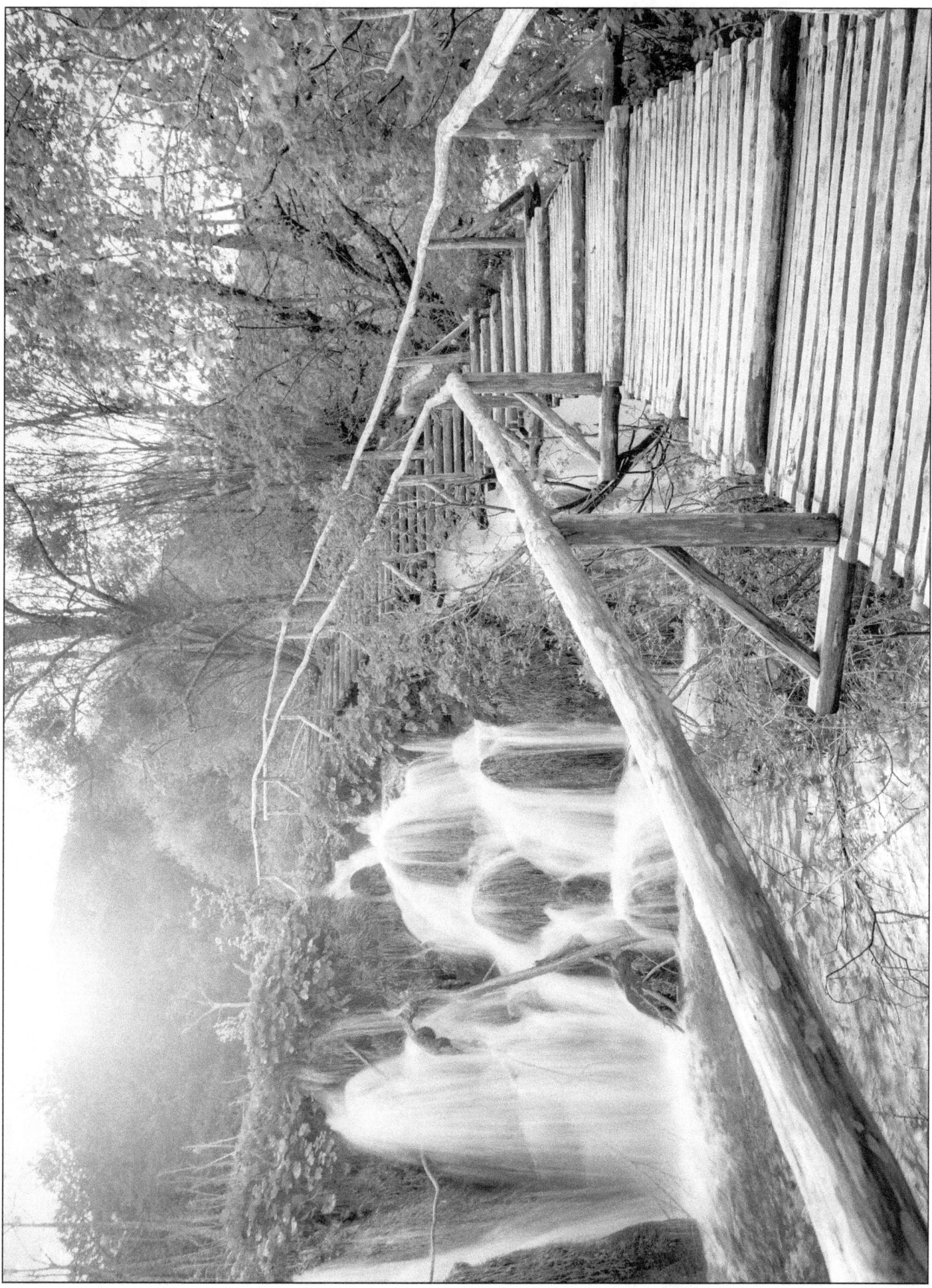

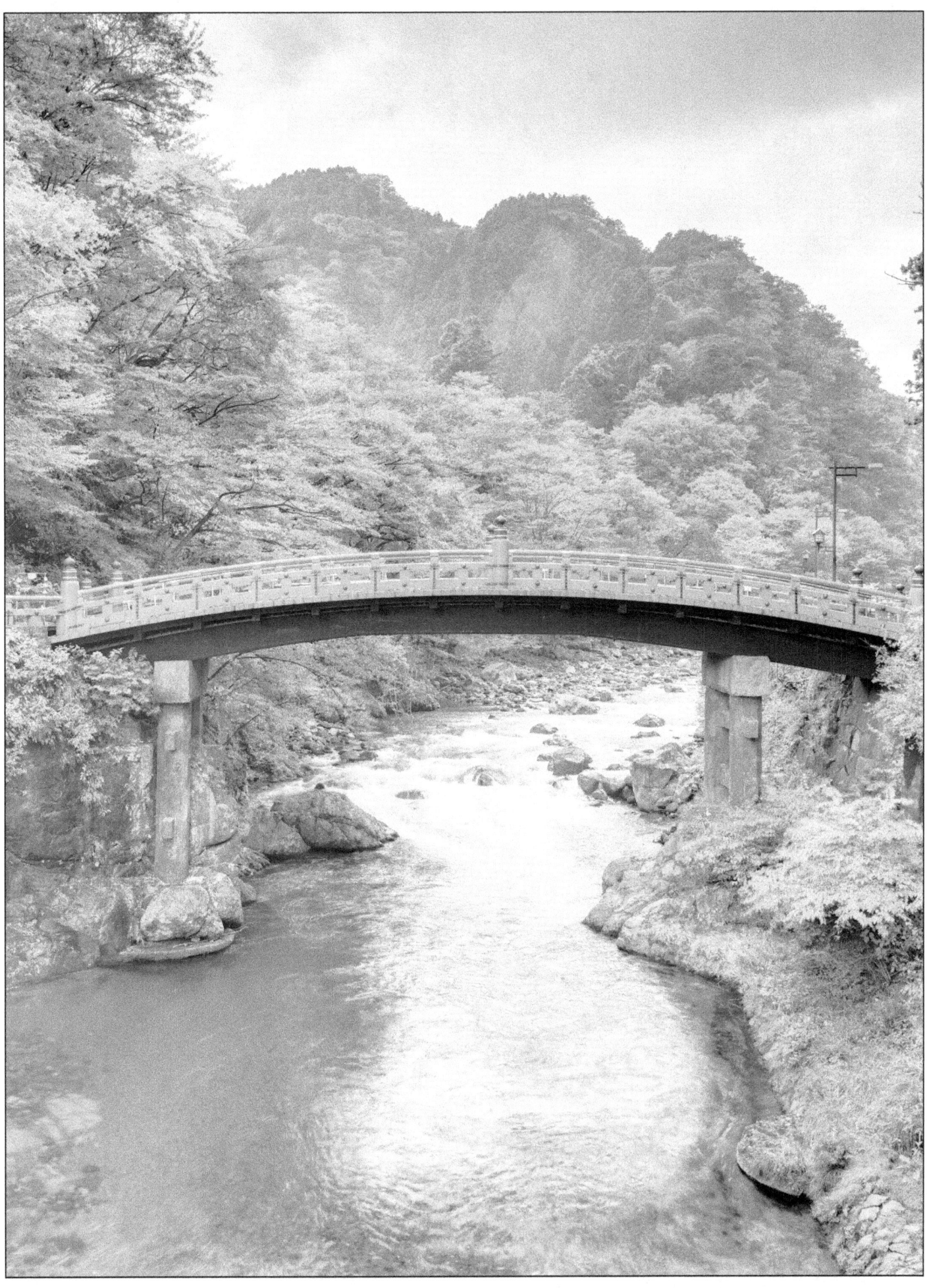

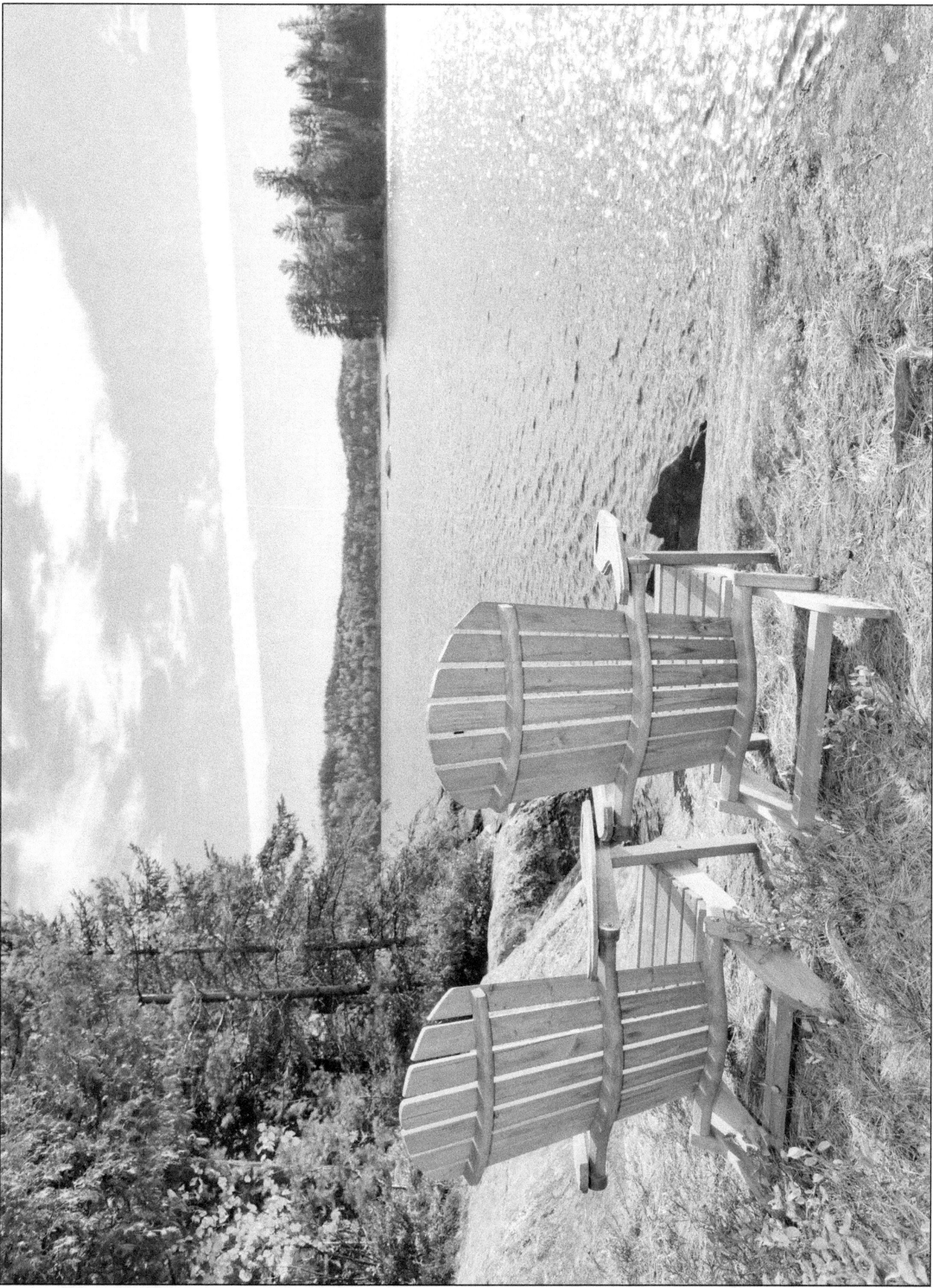

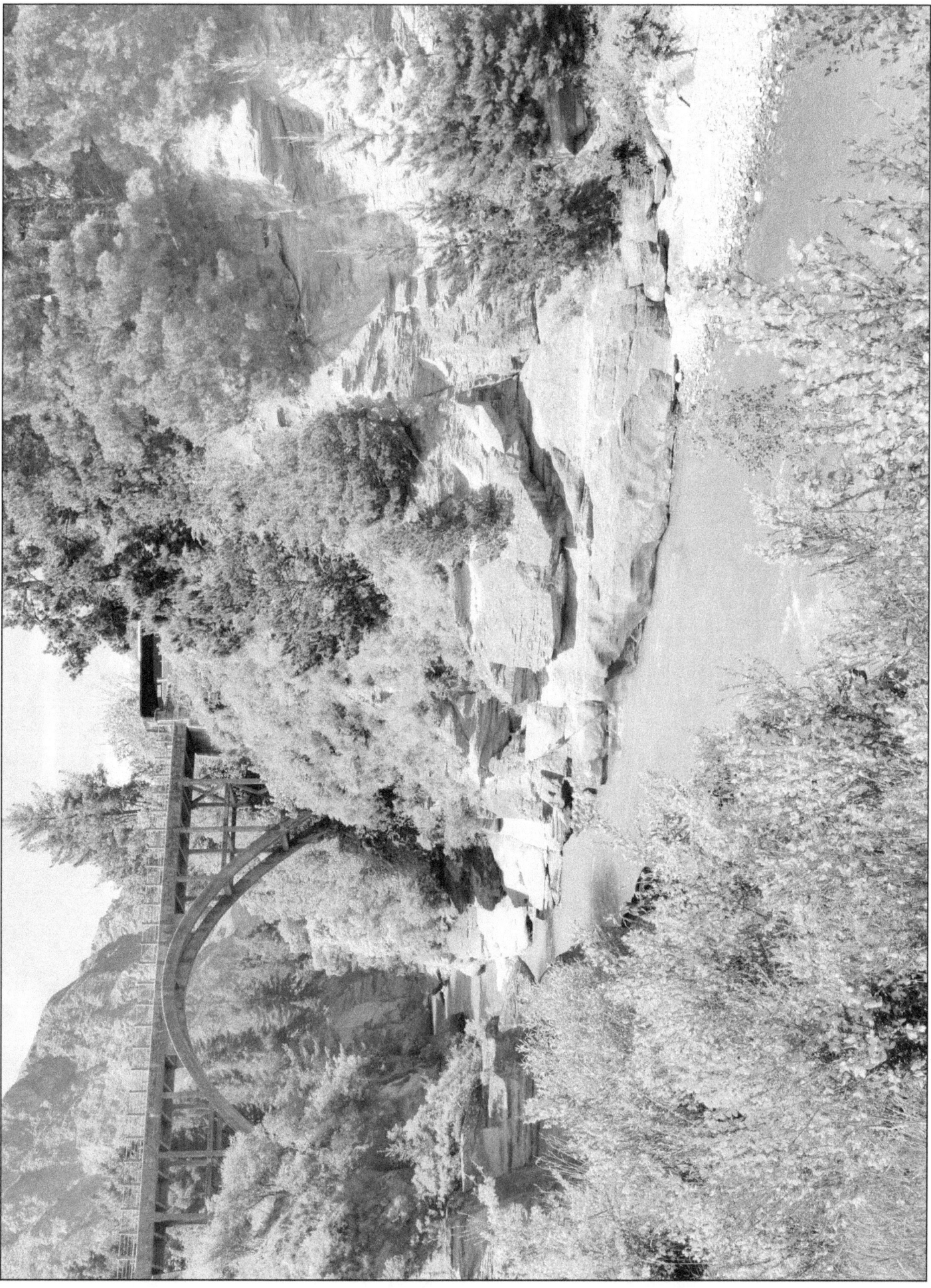

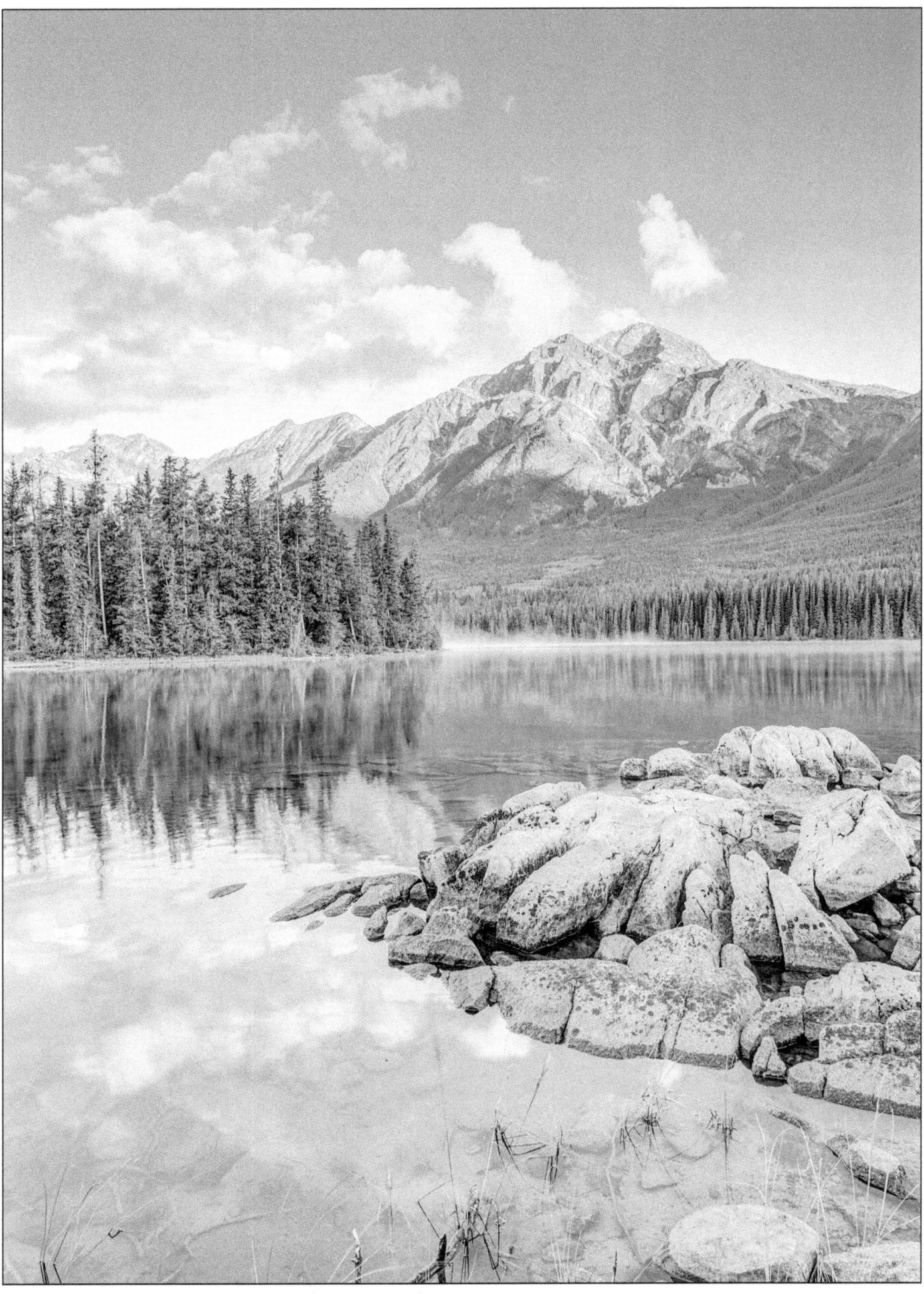

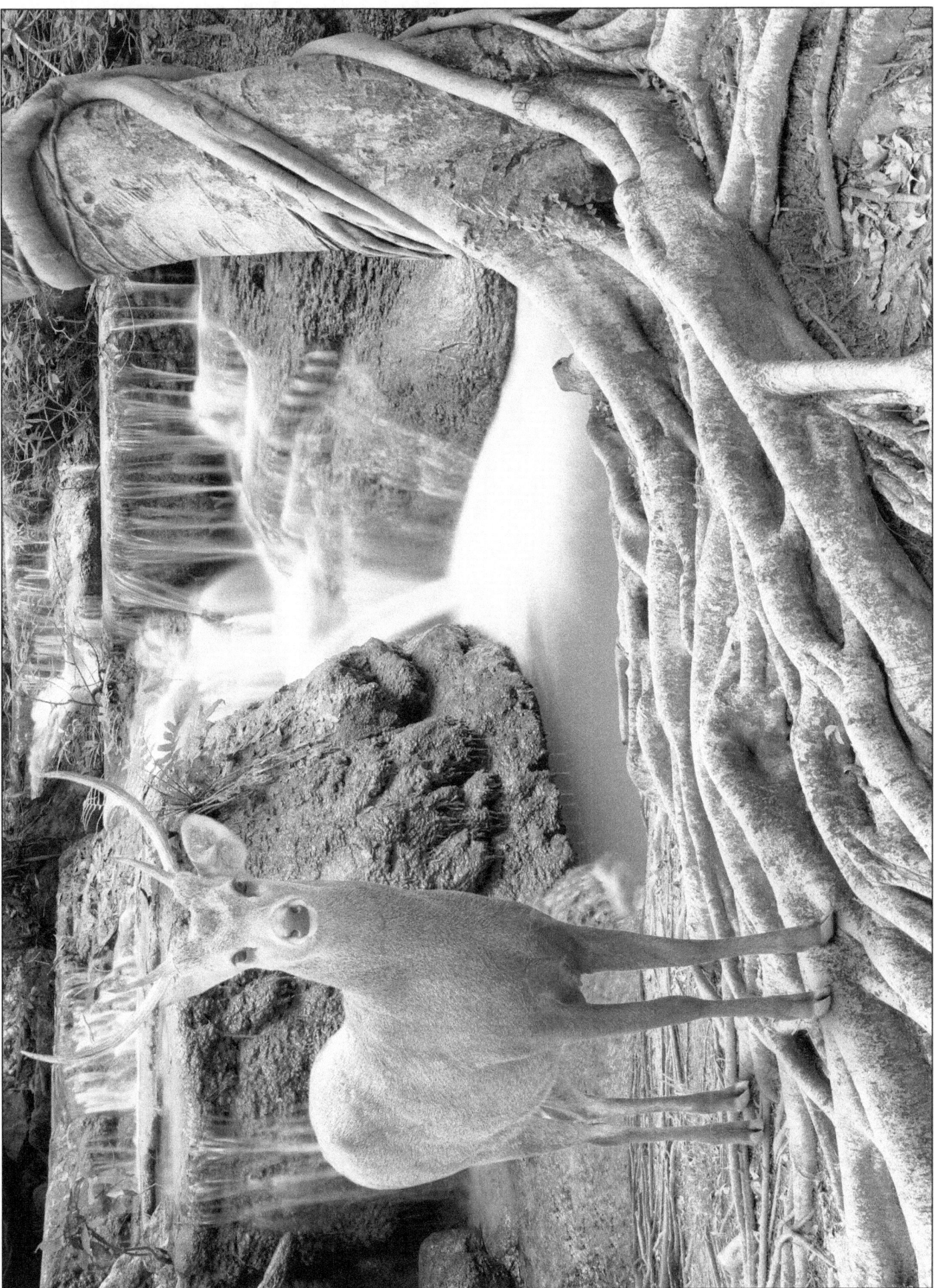

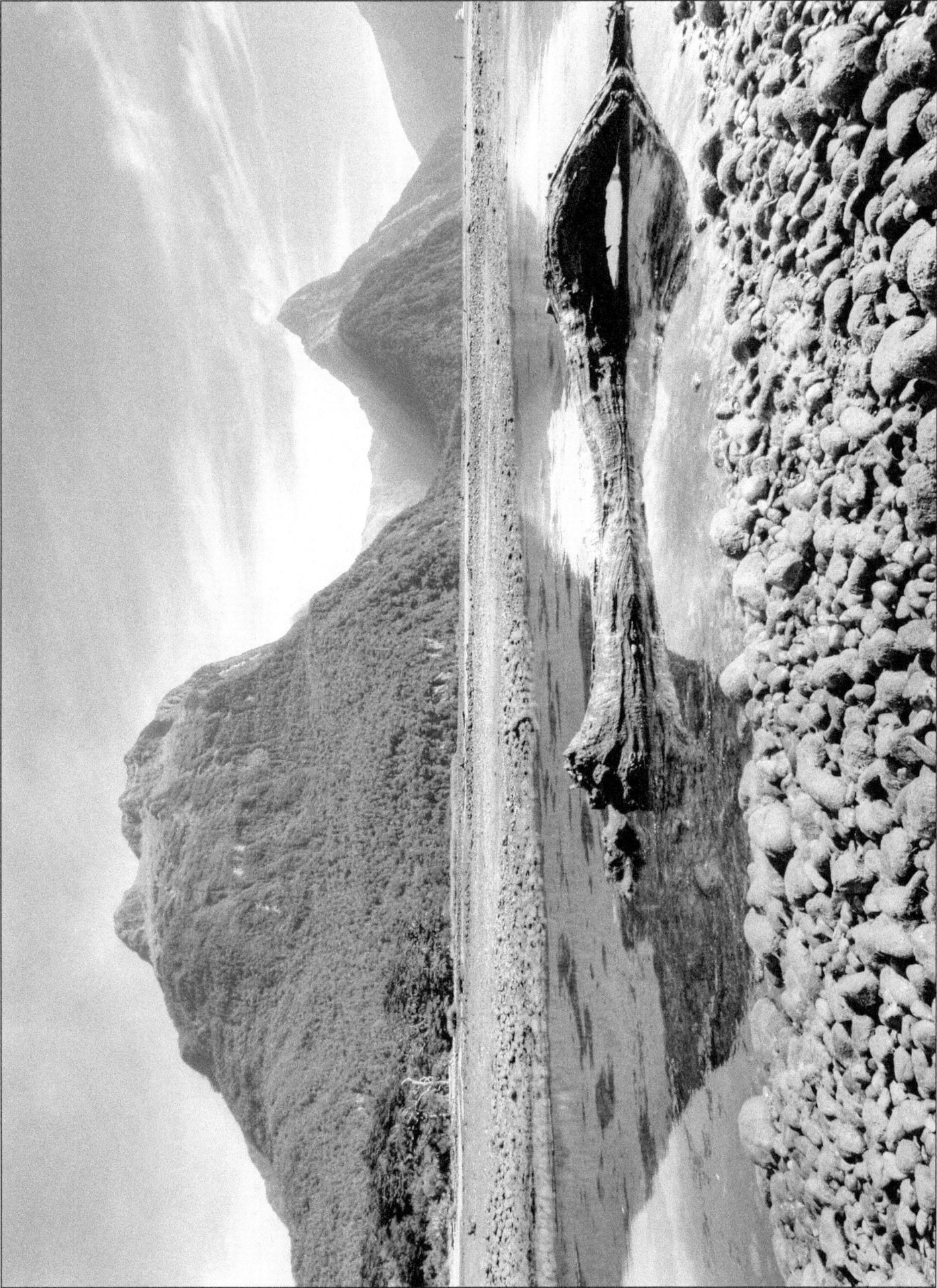

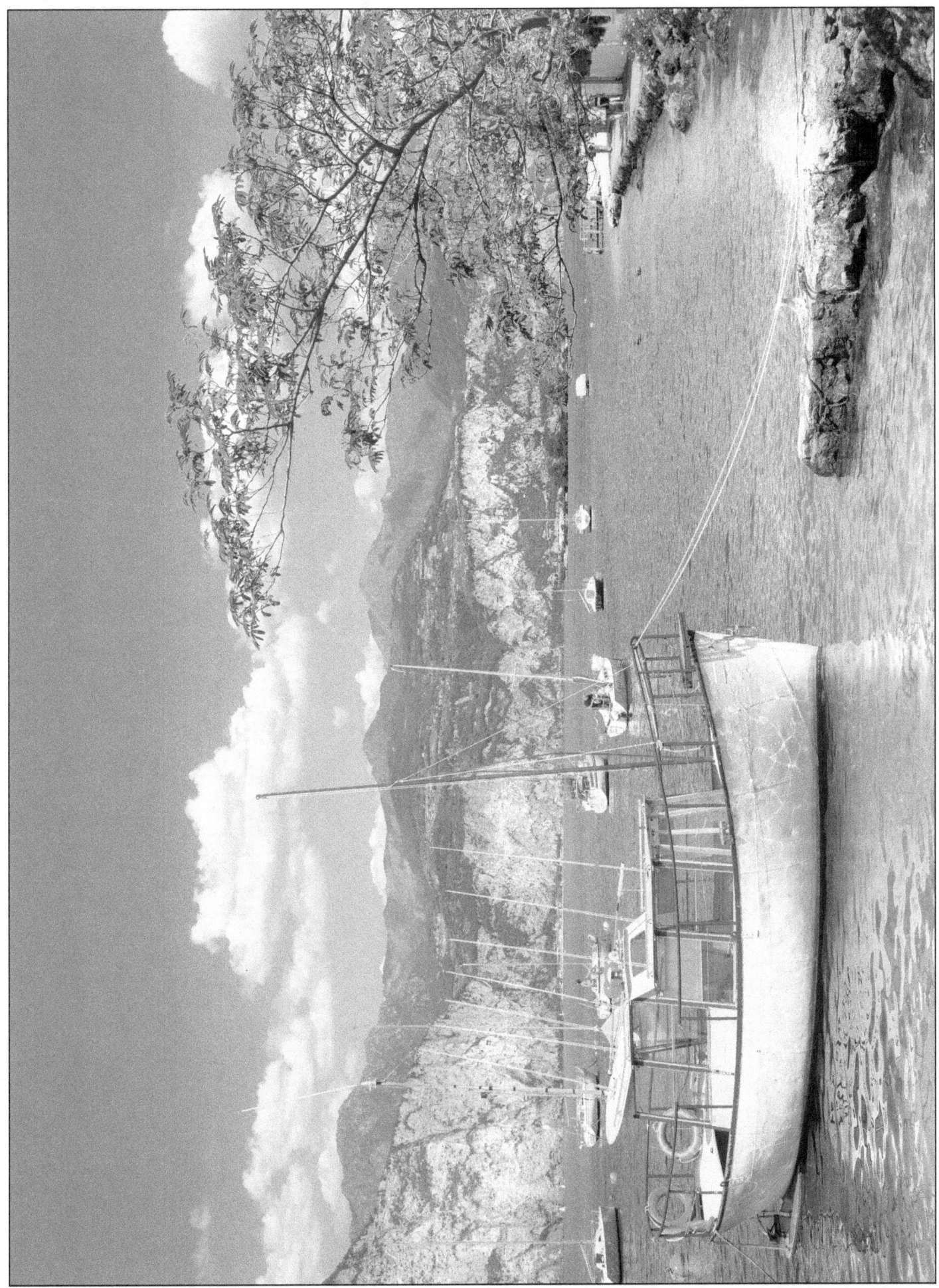

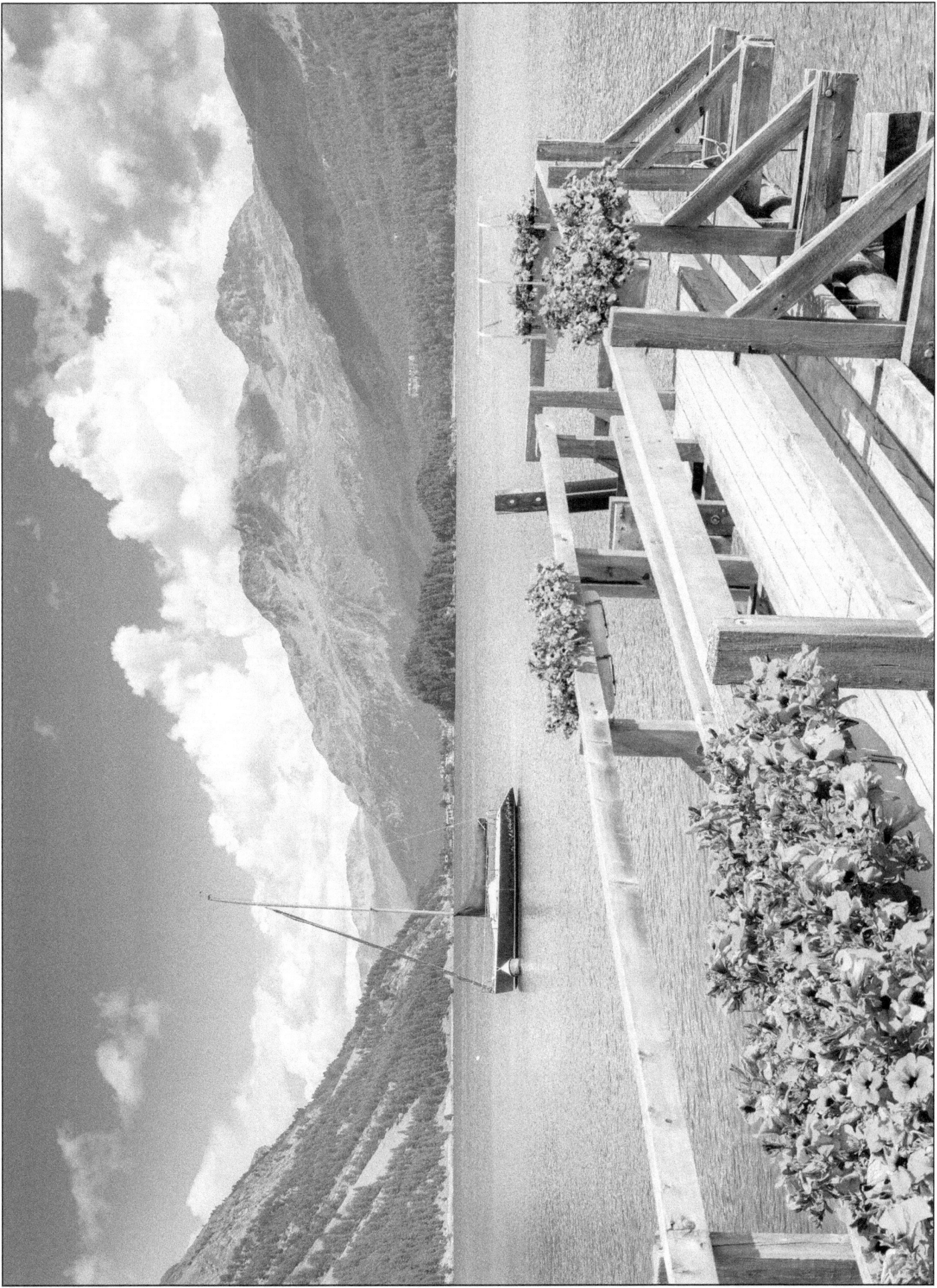

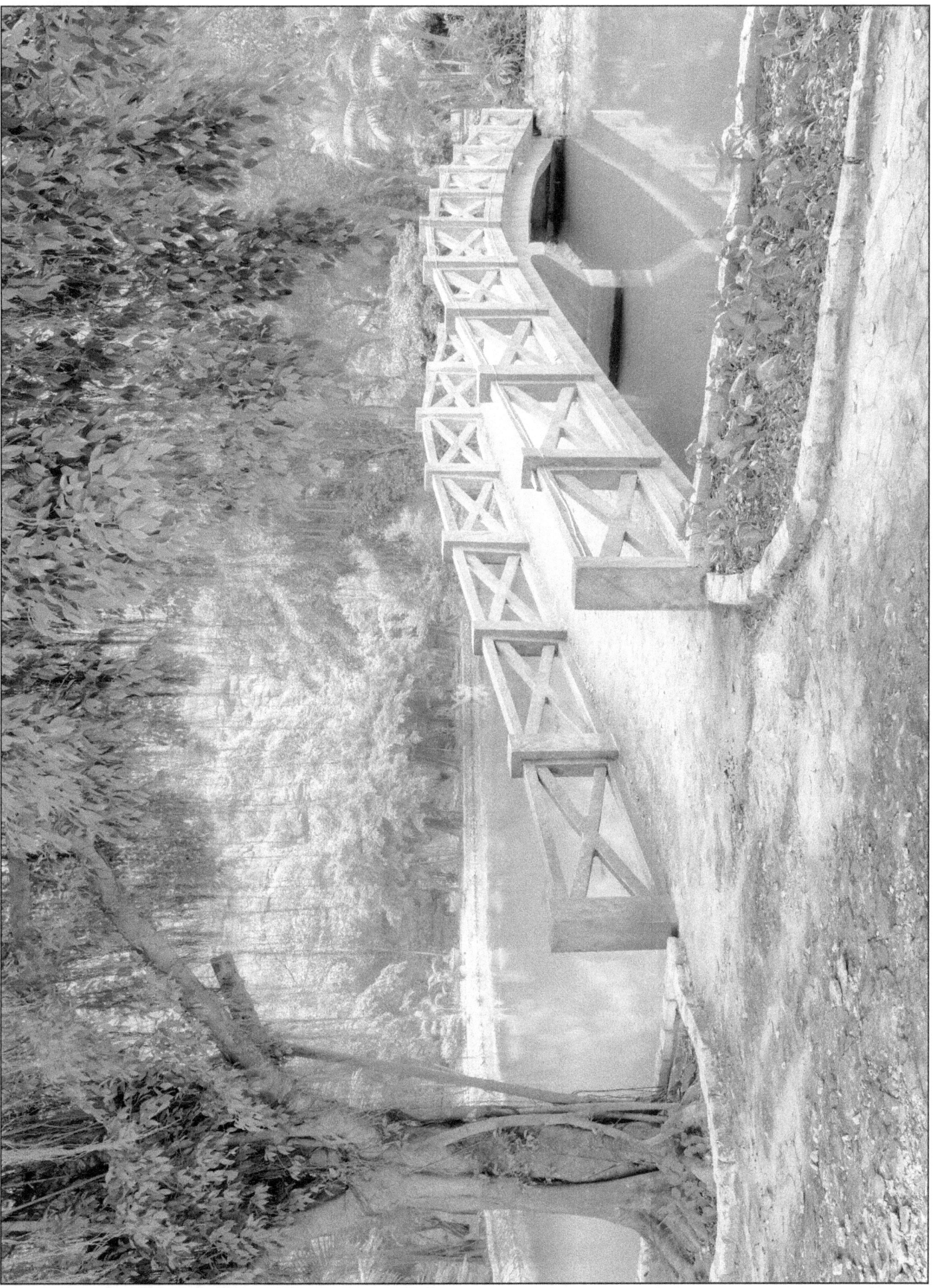

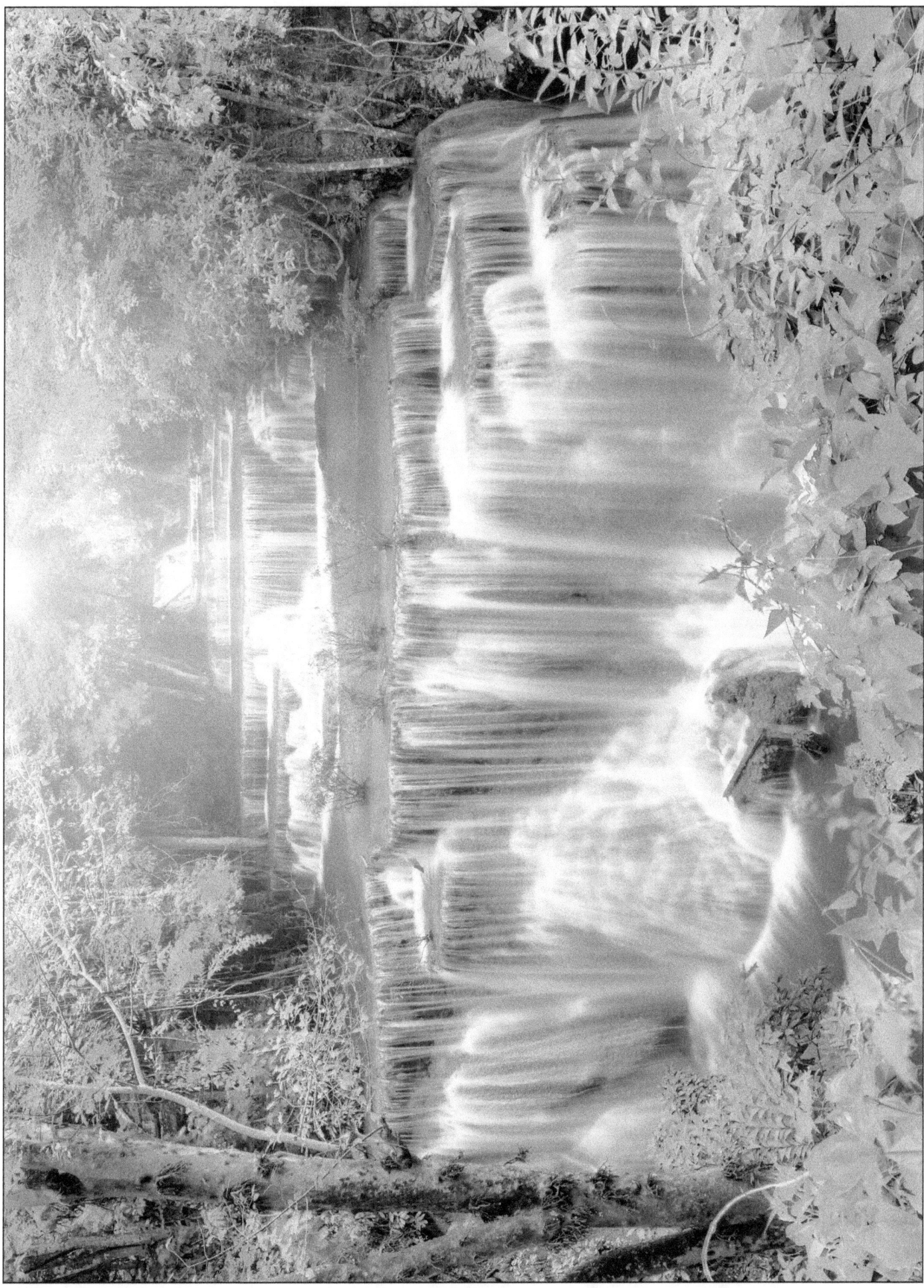

# FREE DOWNLOAD

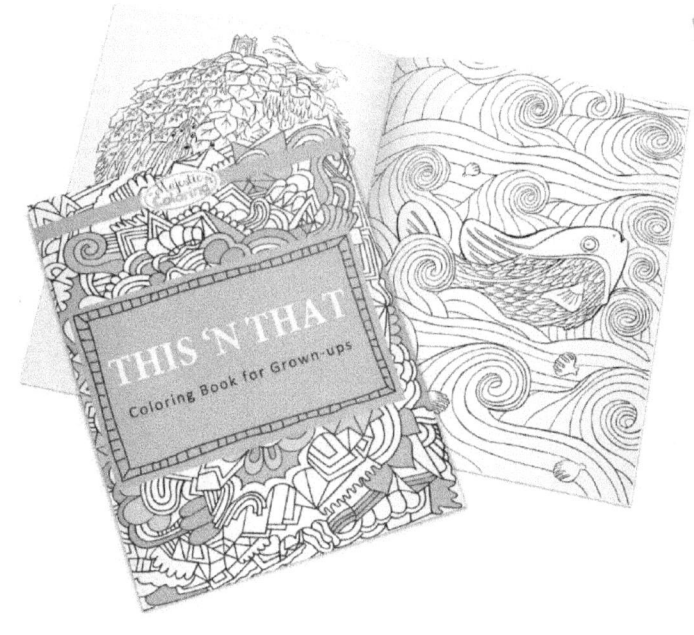

**12** FUN DESIGNS FOR YOUR COLORING ENJOYMENT!

**This 'n That Coloring Book for Grown-Ups** is bundled up in one convenient PDF file to download and print at your leisure.

Sign up for our Majestic Coloring mailing list and get a free copy of **This 'n That Coloring Book for Grown-Ups**.

Click here to get started
http://majesticcoloring.com/thisnthat-free

www.ingramcontent.com/pod-product-compliance
Lightning Source LLC
Chambersburg PA
CBHW080604190526
45169CB00007B/2877